Because You're Worth It

Self-Love Journal Prompts for Loving Who You Are

By: Cassandra Mack

Because You're Worth It

Self-Love Journal Prompts for Loving Who You Are

By: Cassandra Mack

Published by: Strategies For Empowered Living Inc.

About the Author …Cassandra Mack

 Cassandra Mack, MSW is a trained social worker, corporate trainer, and an ordained minister. She is the CVO of *Strategies for Empowered Living Inc.*, a New York based training and development which provides workshops, professional develop coaching and consulting to help individuals and organizations build capacity and facilitate success. For more information about *Strategies For Empowered Living* go to: **StrategiesForEmpoweredLiving.com**

Cassandra is the founder of, **Cassandra Mack Ministries**, a ministry that utilizes print and social media to train, mentor and equip people of faith with Bible-based empowerment tools to unlock the kingdom within and navigate life with grace. Every Sunday Minister Mack hosts *Church By Phone,* where hundreds of people from all around the country to worship and fellowship by phone. To find out more about our ministry go to: **CassandraMackMinistries.com**

Cassandra speaks at churches, corporations, clubs, and national conferences. She has written over 15 books that are widely utilized in the human service sector. Cassandra is the voice of counsel to thousands around the world through her books, seminars, international conference calls, Facebook Pages, YouTube videos and coaching programs.

Connect On Social Media

YouTube.com/CassandraMackChannel

Instagram.com/TheCassandraMack

Facebook.com/Groups/CassandraMackMinistries

Contents

Introduction

Are you overly critical of yourself? Do you have a tough time quieting that inner voice inside your head that tries to eat away at your confidence and make you believe that who you are is not enough? *Have you ever compared yourself to someone else and wished you could be more like them? ...* YOU ARE NOT ALONE. There's a collective human experience that affects so many of us. It's the belief that who we are is not enough. And it's this pervasive feeling of, *"not enoughness,"* that causes us to walk through life feeling inadequate and insecure.

Self-love is a funny thing in that most people know that loving yourself and being okay with who you are authentically is the foundation for happiness, and healthy self-esteem. Yet, so many of us struggle to loves ourselves. That's where this journal comes in. The, **Because You're Worth It Journal,** provides powerful journal prompts that correspond with the 25 components of self-love that are necessary to develop a healthy, self-affirming relationship with one's self.

It's easy to fall into patterns of self-doubt and self-sabotage when we haven't learned to cultivate the 25 essential components that encompass self-love and that empower us to love ourselves from the inside out. Self-love is all about developing a self-appreciating mindset, embracing your authenticity, being compassionate with yourself and letting go of faulty beliefs that undermine your confidence. The **Because You're Worth It Journal** is packed with lots of actionable exercises and self-esteem building tips to help you center yourself in self-love so that you never forget how amazing you are and you learn to appreciate yourself at every stage of life.

It goes without saying that in order to truly love yourself you have to have a healthy relationship with yourself. This comes about by spending time getting to know YOU. But the truth is, most people spend more time investing in their relationships with others than they spend investing in themselves. This is a problem. Why? Because in order to show up for others from a full and resilient place, you have to have a strong and healthy relationship with yourself. Through the 25 components of self-love presented in this journal, you will discover how to do just that.

The **Because You're Worth It Journal**, was written to help you breakthrough the emotional clutter of feeling like who you are is "not enough" so that you can shift into a more self-actualized version of yourself and vibrate at a higher level of confidence. Here's the other piece: If ever you were to share your self-love journey with people who don't mind being transparent, you'll come to realize how much everyone is struggling with the idea of "not being enough," ...regardless of how they look, how successful they appear and how they carry themselves.

Truth is ...You deserve to be loved unconditionally, by the most important person in your life — **YOU**! *Because you're worth it!!!* What this journal will do for you is, help you become more intentional about loving yourself completely, unconditionally and unapologetically. Because when you love yourself …I mean truly love yourself …you make your well-being a top priority and you do your best to show up for life as your most authentic self.

The 25 components of self-love are essential for building a loving, supportive and compassionate relationship with one's self. The **Because You're Worth It Journal**, will help you cultivate and strengthen your skills and capacity in each of these areas.

The relationship that you have with yourself is the longest relationship you'll ever have. It sets the precedent for every other relationship you'll ever have including your relationships… on your job, your friendships, your family, your romantic relationships, your children if you're a parent, your relationship with food, your relationship with money and even your relationship with God.

Genuine self-love is not based on what you look like, your social status, your education and income or how many followers you have on social media. Self-love is about how you feel about YOU on the inside. It's about learning to enjoy your own company and knowing your worth as a human being with your own thoughts, ideas, idiosyncrasies and unique personality.

A lot of people mistakenly confuse self-pampering *(getting your hair & nails done or spending the day at the spa)* and self-indulgence *(treating yourself to your favorite things)* with self-love. These are components of self-care, but self-love goes so much deeper than: taking a bubble bath, or lighting scented candles, or getting a stylish make-over. Self-love is about **knowing who you are at the core**, **being compassionate with yourself, having clear boundaries, advocating for yourself when necessary and loving yourself at every stage of your life!**

As you consciously cultivate the 25 characteristics of self-love presented in this journal, you'll begin to notice how mindful you're becoming about centering yourself in self-love. Remember - journaling is a judgment free space to write about who you are, what's on your mind and what you desire in the deepest part of your heart. Putting your thoughts on paper improves clarity and self-awareness. Journaling gives you a break from the noise of social media, other people's opinions and the many distractions that seek to get your attention. This enables you to tap into your own intuitive wisdom and internal knowing. The **Because You're Worth It** journal provides you with a personal musing space to self-reflect and embrace how awesome you already are. Happy Journaling!

A Foundation for Self-Love

In my opinion, the foundation for healthy self-love comes from how the Bible defines love in 1 Corinthians 13: 4-8. This is a popular Bible verse that speaks to how we ought to love one another. However, this scripture isn't only reserved for how we ought to love other people. In fact, this same kind of love can be applied to how we love and treat ourselves. Unconditional self-love is the starting point for loving others in a healthy way. Let's look at this bible verse so that we can draw some insights about how to love ourselves.

1 Corinthians 13: 4-8 (NIV) ...."4 Love is patient, love is kind. It does not envy, it does not boast, it is not proud. 5 It does not dishonor others, it is not self-seeking, it is not easily angered, it keeps no record of wrongs. 6 Love does not delight in evil but rejoices with the truth. 7 It always protects, always trusts, always hopes, always perseveres. 8 Love never fails. "

1.) Love Is Patient
A big part of developing unconditional self-love involves being patient with yourself. Like every other human on this planet, you are a work in progress so it's important that you learn to be patient with yourself and that you give yourself grace when it comes to your struggles, setbacks, mistakes and imperfections. Just as God is patient with us because He loves us, when have a healthy love for ourselves we are able to extend patience to ourselves and not judge ourselves so harshly for being imperfect human beings. Not only that, when we are patient with ourselves, we are better able to be patient with others because as we develop the fruit or discipline of patience we realize that no one is perfect.
- *What can you do to be more patient with yourself from this day forward?*

2.) Love Is Kind
Do you ever find yourself taking care of everyone else at the expense of your own wellbeing? If yes, this isn't a very kind thing to do to yourself. Do you tend to let people walk all over you and neglect to set godly boundaries? This is not a kind thing to do to yourself either. Part of healthy self-love involves making sure that you are taking good care of yourself and investing in your own self-care so that you can stay mentally well, emotionally healthy, physically well, joyful and peaceful.
- *What can you do to be kinder to yourself from this day forward?*

3.) Love Does Not Envy
Have you ever looked at someone else's life and wish you could be more like them? This is how envy begins. The good news is when you spend time building a better frame of mind and recharging your spirit by spending time with God in

prayer, you grow in confidence and start seeing your own gifts, talents and purpose which over time wards off feelings of envy.

- *What can you do to focus more on your gifts and blessings from this day forward?*

4.) Love Does Not Boast, Love Is Not Proud

Gratitude and humility are great ways to guard your heart against haughtiness or pride. Guarding your heart against pride is not about having fake humility, it's about recognizing that everything you have is a gift from God and that your life is not only about you but about others too. One way to understand humility is not thinking less of yourself, but thinking of yourself less.

- *What can you do to express greater gratitude and humility from this day forward?*

5.) Love Does Not Dishonor

On a scale of 1 to 10 how honorable is your self-talk? Especially when you mess up? Do you say things like, "I'm so stupid," or "I'll never be good enough, or "Everybody hates me"? Whenever you talk to yourself like this, you are dishonoring yourself with your own words. Instead of allowing self-defeatist self-talk to run rampant in your mind, get in the habit of speaking God's Word over yourself so that you learn to change your internal dialogue to one that is more honorable towards yourself. Change your self-talk to statements like: "I am fearfully and wonderfully made." (Psalm 139.14) "I am the head and not the tail" (Deuteronomy 28: 13) "I can do all things through Christ who strengthens me" (Philippians 4: 13) You can also pick up a copy of my book, *Speaking Life Into Your I Am*," which offers bible-based affirmations for building godly confidence.

- *What can you do to be more honorable towards yourself from this day forward?*

6.) Love Is Not Self-Seeking

There's a big difference between loving yourself completely and being self-seeking. When you are self-seeking it's about not caring about who gets hurt as long as you have your way and get what you want. But when you love and care about yourself from a godly place, you also treat others with integrity.

- *What can you do to guard your heart against being self-seeking from this day forward?*

7.) Love Is Not Easily Angered

One of the most unloving things that we can do to ourselves spiritually and psychologically, is to get worked up about things that we have no control over, or allow bitterness and resentment to eat away at our peace of mind and joy. Part of proactive self-love is being intentional about not allowing people, situations and circumstances to rob you of your inner peace.

- *What can you do to become more intentional about not letting anger fester inside of you and eat away at your mental and emotional wellbeing?*

8.) Love Keeps No Record of Wrongs

Do you constantly ruminate over all the mistakes you've made? Do you live under a grey cloud of condemnation? This is not a very loving way to treat yourself. Instead of keeping a running record of all the mess-ups and mistakes you've made, give yourself grace on your past mistakes and don't let them define who you are. Instead remind yourself that God has already forgiven you and sees you as righteous. (1 John 1: 19)

- What can you do to give yourself grace when you make mistakes from this day forward?

9.) Love Does Not Delight in Evil but Rejoices with the Truth

Whenever we take pleasure in the next person's downfall this says a lot about how we feel about ourselves. When we rejoice at the misfortunes of others, it's usually because we are not happy with where we are in our own lives. When you can wholeheartedly be happy for others, it opens a pathway for you to rejoice in your own life. When we have a healthy sense of self-love we can celebrate when somebody else wins.

- What can you do to be more intentional about rejoicing when others rejoice?

10.) Love Protects

Part of healthy self-love involves protecting your peace of mind and your joy. When you love and respect yourself, you protect what's important to you.

- What can you do to be more intentional about preserving your joy and peace?

11.) Love Trusts

Do you trust your own intuitive wisdom? Do you trust your instincts? God has given us instincts, intuition and discernment for a reason – to make better decisions. Part of developing a more loving relationship with yourself is learning to trust yourself.

- What can you do to learn to trust your intuitive wisdom more from this day forward?

12.) Love Hopes

What do you feel hopeful about? According to the Bible's definition of love, Hope is a part of love. Proverbs 13: 12 in the Bible says that hope deferred makes the heart sick. Meaning - when we feel hopeless about our lives and when we give up on our hopes and dreams, it affects our psychological health.

- What can you do to feel more hopeful about your life from this day forward?

13.) Love Perseveres

A big part of healthy self-love is perseverance. You've got to keep on keeping on. Never give up on yourself, no matter how many challenges you face. Remind yourself that God has plans to prosper you and give you hope and a future. (Jeremiah 29: 11) Let the Jeremiah 29: 11 promise inspire you to keep pressing, keep pushing, keep praying.

- What can you do to keep on persevering from this day forward?

And remember, love never fails, So as long as you keep on keeping on until you take your last breath you can never fail at loving yourself

The 25 Components of Self-Love

1.
Self-Knowledge

Self-knowledge is the starting point for authentic self-love. Just think about someone you love. I'll bet you know them very well. You probably know just about everything about them – from their taste in music, to their biggest goals, wildest dreams and even some of the things that they're insecure and fearful about. Reason being is loving someone starts with getting to know them and accepting them for who they are. Similarly, in order to truly love yourself, you have to know *yourself* so that you can love yourself just the way you are.

Write Down 3 Things That You Know About Yourself

1. *I know that I...*

2. *I know that I...*

3. *I know that I...*

ALL ABOUT ME

NAME:
_____

AGE
_____

TODAY'S DATE:
_____

Use these sentence starters to write a brief article about yourself:

- One thing that's important to know about me is...

_____
_____
_____

- What I know you'll appreciate about me is...

_____
_____
_____

- I would love to have the opportunity to...

_____
_____
_____

- I never expected in a million years that I would...

_____
_____
_____

Write Down 4 Things (In Pencil) That You'd Like To Change About Yourself

1

2

3

4

Look over the list of things that you would like to change about yourself and see which things are worth embracing instead of changing. Erase the items off your list that you need to learn to embrace instead of change. As you blow the remainder of these things off of the page, with each bit of residue from the eraser; picture yourself surrendering these things to God, so that you can embrace who you are without condemning yourself for simply being YOU.

Today I choose to embrace these things about myself.

_____

_____

_____

_____

_____

_____

_____

_____

_____

_____

_____

_____

♥ "I will praise You, for I am fearfully and wonderfully made and marvelous are Your works and this my soul knows very well." **Psalm 139: 14**

2
Self-Like

Liking yourself is the pre-requisite for loving yourself. Why? Because you can't truly fall in love with someone unless you like them first. *So let's begin with self-like.*

I don't know about you, but growing up I always felt like I had to work overtime to get people to like me. *Have you ever felt this way?* Like most people, I wanted to fit in and be accepted. But I now realize that all of my ill-fated attempts to try to get others to accept me, were actually a reflection of what I needed to accept in myself. I needed to learn how to like myself and become more accepting of ALL OF ME… including what made me different.

Self-like comes from embracing all of the different aspects of you – your great characteristics as well as your not-so-great points. This includes: your quirks, unique personality traits, talents, strengths insecurities, doubts, your body, how you show up for your relationships and even the things that you're not 100% satisfied with. You might be dissatisfied with certain parts of yourself. *Who isn't?* …But all of your parts make up the whole of WHO YOU ARE. Therefore, all of these attributes are aspects of yourself that you need to embrace and care for.

Self-like can start with the tiniest of steps like acknowledging to yourself that you've come a long way, or that there's even just one part of your life that you truly appreciate or one good thing you did in your life that you are proud of. Liking yourself may not happen overnight, but as you consciously care for yourself in simple yet meaningful ways; what will happen over time is you'll begin to realize that you're a pretty awesome person. And this is a very **BIG STEP** in the right direction.

Write down (in bright colored pens) 3 things that you like about yourself.

 I like...

1.

2.

3.

Write Down 3 Things That You Are Proud Of Doing, Learning, or Overcoming

Here's One Thing That I Am Proud Of

Here's Something Else I Am Proud Of

Here's One More Thing That I Am Proud Of

3
Self-Confidence

Self-confidence is like the gorilla glue to self-love, in that it serves as the mental adhesive to keep you together, when it seems like your world is falling apart. A big part of developing self-confidence is recognizing what's already working in your life by identifying all of the things that make you realize ...**You've Got This!!!** So, here's what you're going to do: You are going to create a **What's Already Working In My Life List**.

Once you see on paper what you've already got going for yourself and start to realize that you were the one who had the confidence, creativity & motivation to make it happen, it will ignite the necessary spark of self-confidence that will serve to remind you to... *BELIEVE IN YOURSELF*, whenever self-doubt tries to come for your confidence.

HERE'S WHAT'S ALREADY wOrKING IN MY LIFE

♥ Therefore, do not throw away your confidence, which has a great reward."
Hebrews 10: 35

4
Self-Compassion

Inside of every adult there's a little wounded child trying to take care of itself. And until you begin to actively engage with that part of yourself and start seeing them, caring for them and figuring out what he/she needs to feel loved and cared for; it will be difficult to fully embrace the man or woman you've evolved into today.

Self-compassion is the practice of being kind and empathetic towards yourself; so that when the wounded part of you emerges and acts out in ways that leave you feeling powerless, regretful, ashamed or vulnerable; you can figure out how to best take care of yourself. You may not realize it, but that part of you is trying to tell YOU something about your "Self". *What is your inner child trying to tell you now that you're all grown up & fully capable of giving yourself the things that you need to be well and thrive?*

Finish this sentence

✍ The inner child in me is trying to tell me that ...

_____

_____

_____

_____

_____

_____

_____

_____

_____

_____

_____

_____

_____

_____

_____

_____

_____

_____

_____

_____

_____

_____

_____

_____

_____

_____

_____

_____

_____

_____

_____

_____

_____

_____

_____

_____

_____

_____

_____

_____

_____

_____

_____

Simple Ways That I Can Take Care of The Child Within Whenever That Person Emerges

Here Are Some Ways That I Can Care for My Inner Child Whenever He/She Emerges

I can...

I can...

I can...

5
Self-Care

Self-care is any helpful activity that you do in order to take care of yourself mentally, emotionally, spiritually and, or physically. It's the intentional practice of making sure that you are being taken care of by you. Although most people know that it's essential to practice good self-care, many of us overlook it when we need it the most. Good self-care improves our: frame of mind, productivity, relationships, emotional health and our ability to cope with life's challenges. Self-care anchors us spiritually and it aids in reducing the overwhelming effects of stress.

☑ Self-care means recognizing when you are burning yourself out and figuring out what can be done to alleviate stress.

☑ Self-care means getting the sleep you need so that you can rest your body & relax your mind.

☑ Self-care means making sure that you're eating well, drinking enough water and exercising.

☑ Self-care involves knowing what your values and boundaries are and then being intentional about maintaining them.

☑ Self-care involves giving some thought to what you need to be healthy, happy, fulfilled and whole and then doing more of those things that support your positive productivity and overall well-being.

Think of At Least 3 Things That You Can Do To Take Care of Yourself & Jot Them Down In The Speech Bubble. **I can....**

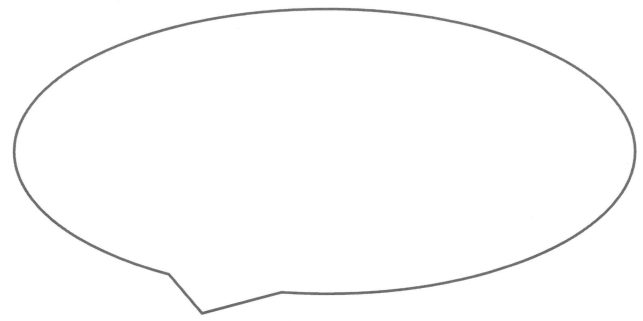

6
Self-Worth

Self-worth means having positive regard for yourself for no other reason than you are a human being who has the right to life, liberty, justice and the pursuit of happiness. Self-worth is about knowing that your life matters in the grand scheme of this world because you are a person who was created with a mind of your own and a purpose to fulfil. Self-worth is about realizing that you are a worthy human being deserving of a life that is characterized by dignity, respect and personal volition.

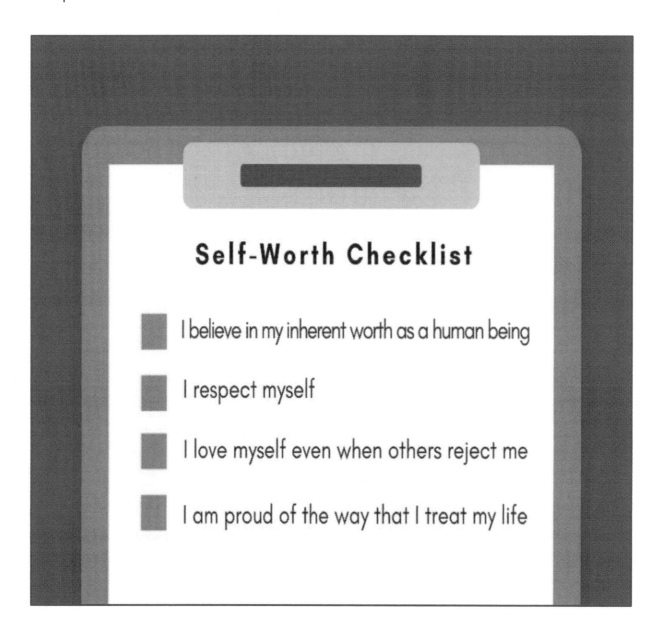

Self-Worth Checklist

- ☐ I believe in my inherent worth as a human being
- ☐ I respect myself
- ☐ I love myself even when others reject me
- ☐ I am proud of the way that I treat my life

SELF-WORTH CHECKLIST

Write down 5 things that you can do starting today to anchor yourself in your own self-worth.

I can ...

-
-
-
-
-

7
Self-Dignity

Dignity refers to your inherent value as a human being. Dignity transcends all of our differences, putting our common identity as human beings above all of the things that seek to divide us as a human race.

Dignity is the glue that holds all of our relationships together and forms the foundation for respect because it speaks to the universal notion that it is every human being's intrinsic desire: to be seen, heard, and treated justly; to be recognized and understood.

Create 3 self-dignity rules for yourself that you will do your best to abide by so you can anchor yourself in your self-dignity.

1. I will do my best to never allow myself to get to the point where I accept...

2. I will do my best to never allow anyone to ever think for a second that it's okay to ...

3. I will do my best to make sure that I anchor myself in my dignity by...

8
Self-Respect

Self-respect is the foundation for: every decision you'll ever make, how you treat yourself, and how you allow others to treat you. While dignity is about what you believe, self-respect is demonstrated by your choices & your conduct. Self-respect is established by developing personal standards that are demonstrated by conducting yourself with self-regard, integrity, and dignity.

Write Down 3 Songs That You Like That Embody A Message of Self-Respect

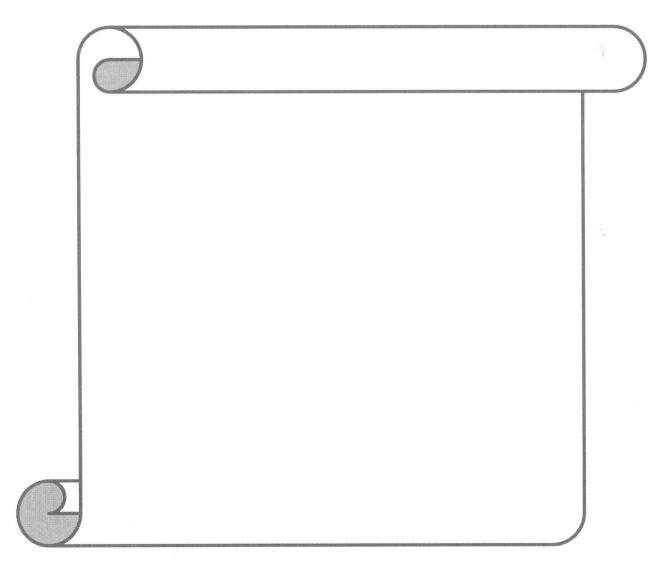

My Self-Respect Do's & Don'ts

I DO	I DON'T	I DO	I DON'T

9
Self-Awareness

Having self-awareness means that you have a keen understanding and accurate awareness of your personality. This includes your strengths and weaknesses, thoughts and beliefs, emotions, habits, how your behavior affects others and even your emotional triggers. Having self-awareness helps you to not only understand your motives and what makes you tick, but it also helps you better understand how you come across to others.

Things That I Am Keenly Aware of About Myself

I know that I am...

I know that I can be...

I know that sometimes I tend to be a bit...

☑ To increase your self-awareness, ask people whom you trust and who know you well to give you some honest feedback, on different aspects of yourself. This could be about your habits, the things you talk about a lot, how you interact with others or even things they notice about you that you might not be aware of. This may help you learn something about yourself that you would otherwise not be aware of.

Write Down 1 Thing That You Learned About Yourself As A Result of The Feedback

10
Self-Growth

Self-growth also known as personal growth/personal development is a process of spiritual, mental, and emotional development that lasts a lifetime. Self-growth is an ongoing process of learning and developing new skills, habits and mindsets that enable you to become a stronger, better, wiser version of yourself.

The beauty of personal growth is that the possibilities for you are endless. As you continue to grow as a person, you will embark on an extraordinary and meaningful path in life that will lead you to a stronger, better and wiser version of yourself during each stage of life. It's never too late to grow as a person, even if you are starting your personal development journey for the first time right now.

Below are just a few examples of areas of personal growth. Place a checkmark next to the areas that you would like to work on and jot down any additional areas where you would like to focus on growing as a person.

1. Be More Confident
2. Get Along Better With Others
3. Be Kinder To Yourself
4. Become A More Forgiving Person
5. Eat Better & Exercise More
6. Not Take Everything So Personal
7. Stop Procrastinating
8. Take Action Towards Your Goals
9. Manage Your Time Better
10. Pursue Your Dreams
11. Heal What's Holding You Back Emotionally
12. Other Areas ....

Personal Growth To Do List

11
Self-Forgiveness

Everyone makes mistakes, but learning how to grow from our mistakes, let go, move on, and forgive ourselves is important for one's own well-being. Forgiveness is not about evading responsibility and not being remorseful, instead it means that you accept full responsibility for your actions, you accept responsibility for the hurt or harm that your actions caused, and you are willing to move past it and move on with your life without becoming psychologically paralyzed by a past incident or situation that you cannot change.

> In the center of the cloud **in pencil** write the things that you need to forgive yourself for. Then, erase those things from the cloud. As you blow away the residue of the eraser feel yourself forgiving yourself & releasing these things to God.

♥ "There is no condemnation for those who are in Christ Jesus" **Romans 8: 1**

12
Self-Image

Self-image is the idea, or mental picture that one has of oneself. Self-image can be understood as the person you see yourself as when you look in the mirror and how you picture yourself in your mind.

There are 3 elements that make up a person's self-image. They are:
1. The way you perceive or think of yourself.
2. The way you believe other people view you.
3. The way you would like to be perceived (your ideal self).

It's important to realize that everyone has things about themselves that they may not be 100% satisfied with, but having a positive self-image means that overall, you see yourself in an optimistic light and you have a healthy appreciation for your best qualities.

When you look in the mirror, what kind of person do you see? Finish this sentence. When I see me I see someone who is ....

_____
_____
_____
_____
_____
_____
_____
_____
_____
_____
_____
_____
_____

♥ "So God created mankind in his own image, In the image of God he created them; male and female he created them." **Genesis 1: 27**

Write 3 Words That Describe What You See When You Look In The Mirror

WHO AM I?

You Are Awesome!
You Are Special!
You Are Unique!
You Are Needed!
You Are Loved!

COLUMN A →   **COLUMN B**

This Is Who I Am   This Is Who I Am Not

I AM... _____

I Am... _____

I Am... _____

I Am... _____

I Am... _____

I Am... _____

I Am... _____

I Am... _____

I Am... _____

13
Self-Trust

Self-trust is cultivated when we honor our instincts, intuition and integrity instead of constantly looking to other people to tell us what we should do with our lives. Self-trust comes from trusting the God in you. Self-trust is about trusting your Holy Spirit to discern what's best for you in any given moment in order to guide you towards your ultimate good.

A big part of self-trust means you must stop downplaying and dismissing your inner voice, because you are the only person who will have to live out the consequences of your choices. Not to mention, you are the one person in your life who will be with you in every situation ...every step of the way. If you struggle with self-trust, here are 4 simple ways to build self-trust. After reviewing each method, write down any additional ideas that come to mind for developing self-trust in that particular area.

1. Spend Time With Yourself
Just like any relationship would not be able to cultivate trust if the people in it didn't spend any quality time together, you are going to have difficulty learning to trust yourself unless you spend time getting to know yourself. Write down some things that you can do to know yourself on a deeper level ...your motives, your deepest desires and what makes you tick.

2. Make Time For Regular Self-Care
Just like you would probably have a tough time feeling deeply connected to an intimate partner who did not treat you well, you'll probably struggle to connect with your inner wisdom and gut instincts if you don't take good care of yourself. Self-care enables you to ground yourself emotionally and this helps to build self-trust. Write down a few ways that you can take care of yourself.

3. Set Boundaries

Setting and maintaining clear boundaries is an important aspect of self-trust. When you trust yourself enough to set limits with others and stand up for yourself; you start to develop a higher degree of self-trust. Write down at least 3 personal boundaries that you believe are important to establish for yourself so that other people will know what they can expect from you and so that you are clear on what feels appropriate for you and what does not.

4. Learn To Trust Your Judgment By Clarifying Your Values

If you're not sure whether or not you can trust your own judgment, clarifying your values is a great place to start. When you are clear about what's important to you and why; your values will be the guidepost for your decisions. This will help you to trust your own judgment. Reading the Bible will also help you to trust your judgment, because the Bible provides wisdom for living. Write down at least one thing that you can do to trust your judgment more.

♥ "The Holy Spirit will guide you into all truth." **John 16: 13**

14
Self-Esteem

Self-esteem can be defined as your personal appraisal of your self-worth and value as a person. Self-esteem also encompasses how much you appreciate and like yourself.

Self-esteem plays a substantial role in personal motivation and success. Low self-esteem can hold you back from achieving your life's ambitions, because when your self-esteem is low, you don't believe yourself to be capable of achieving your goals and changing your life for the better. But on the other hand, when you have healthy self-esteem; not only do you believe in your inherent worth as a human being, you also see yourself as a person who is capable of achieving success as defined by you.

Following are some simple ways to tell if you have healthy self-esteem. Circle the ones that apply to you. You probably have healthy self-esteem if you:

- Genuinely like yourself
- Have a healthy appreciation for your best qualities
- Express your needs without feeling guilty
- Set clear boundaries and stand by them
- Feel confident about achieving most of your goals
- Are able to say "no" when it's necessary for you to do so
- Identify your strengths and work on improving your weaknesses
- Confident in your ability to make decisions that serve your highest good
- Able to build secure and healthy relationships
- Are willing to leave a toxic relationship
- Don't allow your imperfections to hold you back
- Do not obsess over what other people think about you
- Do not live your life to please people
- Comfortable being yourself

Are there any areas where you need to work on building healthier self-esteem? Jot them down below.

_____

_____

_____

_____

_____

_____

_____

_____

Five Simple Ways To Start Building Healthier Self Esteem Today

1. Identify and Challenge Your Negative Beliefs

Start becoming more mindful of the negative beliefs that you have about yourself so that you can work on changing your negative beliefs to beliefs that empower you. For example, you might find yourself thinking, "I'll never have a good life" or "No one likes me." When you find yourself thinking in this negative manner, be deliberate about looking for evidence that challenges those beliefs. Write down both the negative statement and your evidence that disproves these kinds of beliefs. Whenever you find yourself ruminating on negative beliefs, refer to your evidence so that you can remind yourself that your negative beliefs are invalid.

2. Identify Your Positive Qualities

Are you reliable, thoughtful, trustworthy, kind? These are all positive qualities that you can refer to in order to start building healthier self-esteem. It's a good idea to write down positive things about yourself, like: your strengths and talents, or nice things that people have said about you. When you start to get down on yourself, use your list of positive qualities to remind yourself that there are good things about you. Positive self-talk is a big part of improving your self-esteem. By identifying your positive qualities, you now have positive things that you can say to yourself about yourself.

3.Try To Catch Yourself When You Fall Back Into Negative Thinking Patterns & Don't Let Yourself Stay There.

When you find yourself reverting back to negative self-talk and self-limiting thinking, catch yourself in the act and remind yourself of your commitment to building better self-esteem. Then, challenge the negative belief with a thought that moves you in the direction of positive self-esteem.

4. Build Positive Relationships and Avoid or Limit Time Spent With Negative People

Make an effort to build relationships with people who lift you up and try to avoid or limit your time with people who try to drag you down.

5. Become More Assertive and Learn to Say No

People with low self-esteem often find it hard to stand up for themselves and say no to others. Because of this, they tend to put other people's needs ahead of their own, even at the expense of their own self-care, priorities and happiness. You have a right to say "no" and you also have a right to speak up for yourself.

15
Self-Efficacy

Self-efficacy refers to your belief in your ability to implement the necessary choices needed to produce the outcomes that you desire to manifest in your life. Self-efficacy includes confidence in one's ability to exert control over one's own motivation, habits, and choices.

Using Past Successes As A Pathway To Stronger Self-Efficacy

You can use past successes to build confidence for self-efficacy. Think about a time in your life when you were able to stick to something that you decided to do. It could be: a change in diet, giving up smoking, an exercise regimen, getting yourself into therapy or something else. Make a list of the things that you did that allowed you to be successful in accomplishing that particular goal.

_____

_____

_____

_____

_____

_____

_____

_____

_____

_____

_____

_____

_____

_____

_____

_____

♥ "I can do all things through Christ who strengthens me." **Philippians 4: 13**

Using Mastery of A Skill As A Pathway To Stronger Self-Efficacy

Another helpful way to build self-efficacy is through recalling the skills that you have already mastered. By recalling the skills that you have already mastered you can now use this information about yourself as a bridge to building a new skill or habit. By bearing in mind past personal accomplishments, you provide yourself with critical information about your potential and your ability to produce positive change in your life.

☑ In the space below, write down as many skills as you can think of that you have already learned and or mastered.

_____

_____

_____

_____

_____

_____

_____

_____

_____

_____

_____

_____

_____

_____

_____

_____

_____

_____

_____

_____

_____

_____

16
Self-Regulation

Self-regulation is the ability to control your impulses as well as monitor and manage your emotions, thoughts, and behaviors in ways that are appropriate for the setting and situation and produce positive results such as: personal well-being, self-control, healthy relationships, and self-awareness.

Self-regulation involves taking a pause between a feeling and an action—taking the time to think things through before reacting or acting on impulse. It also involves making a plan when you feel stressed or upset and being able to wait patiently when waiting is necessary.

People who are skilled at self-regulating tend to have the following abilities. **Circle** the ones that you possess and place a **check mark** next to the abilities that you would like to cultivate.

1. They can calm themselves down when upset
2. They can encourage themselves when feeling sad or disappointed
3. They have healthy communication skills and can express themselves assertively without being negative and aggressive
4. They can persevere during difficult times
5. They try to put forth their best effort
6. They are flexible and can adapt when necessary
7. They can experience feelings of upset without acting out
8. They do not verbally express every thought that they think, especially the negative ones about other people

In the box below write down one action step that you can take to build better self-regulation skills.

17
Self-Expression

Have you ever stopped to think about how you express yourself? How we express ourselves to others forms the basis of our personality as experienced by other people, and sets the tone for other people understanding us. Self-expression is an important aspect of your life to pay attention to, especially if you want to feel like you are showing up for life as your most authentic self and if you want to feel more understood by others.

Although the idea of authentic self-expression seems simple enough, it's not always as easy as it sounds. Why? Because we are so inundated with messages that try to tell us how we should look, think, and act and who we should be, that it can be hard to let go of other people's expectations and just be ourselves. The good news is there are many outlets for self-expression. Some people write and journal their feelings. Some people make art. Some people draw. Some people sing. Some people recite poetry. Some people sew or cook. Some people express themselves through their hair and clothing. There really is no limit to the ways that people express their creativity, individuality and personality.

What are some of the ways that you express yourself?

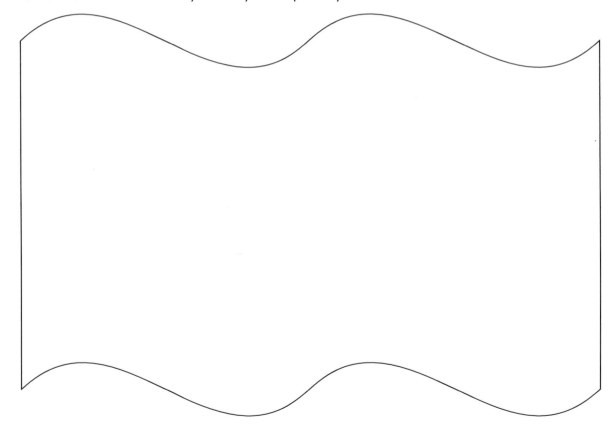

18
Self-Resilience

Resilience is the ability to get back up when life knocks you down. We all face adversity and challenges. Resilience is the ability to adapt and recover whenever we are faced with life-changing situations, and then emerging even stronger than before.

Resiliency Road Map

In the roadmap below, jot down the strengths and qualities that have empowered you to become more resilient; especially when you've had to face difficulties and overcome adversity.

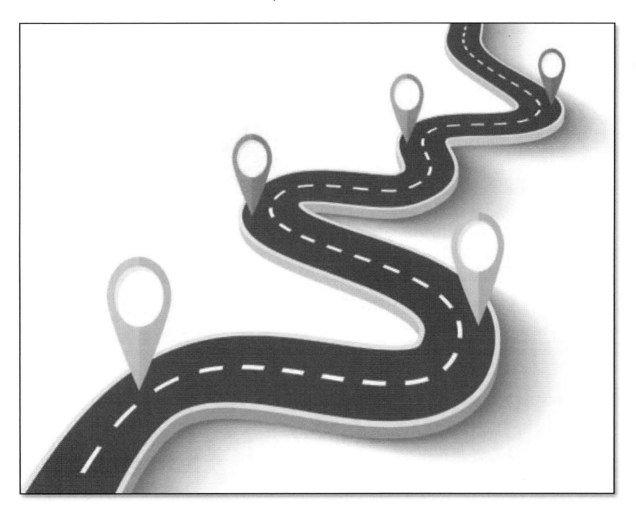

♥ "Seek the Lord & His strength seek His presence continually." **1 Chronicles 16: 11**

19
Self-Mastery

Self-mastery is developed through self-awareness as well as understanding and controlling your thoughts, emotions and actions. Self-mastery is essentially mastering one's own self. Self-mastery begins with having insight and awareness of your own beliefs, values, inclinations and overall personality. It is also the desire to grow mentally, emotionally and spiritually. Self-mastery is knowing yourself inside and out with a resolve to creating the best version of yourself.

Self-mastery is the process of ...

1. **Knowing yourself...** knowing who you are authentically at the core

2. **Creating yourself...** becoming the kind of person that you desire to be

3. **Growing yourself...** developing a growth mindset and knowing that there is always room to grow

4. **Improving yourself...** investing in your personal development

5. **Exceeding yourself...** allowing yourself to evolve mentally, emotionally & spiritually in order to become the next version of yourself

6. **Maintaining yourself...** sustaining the self-work that you've invested in yourself by developing habits and daily disciplines that support the kind of person whom you desire to be

☑ Select at least one area of self-mastery from the previous page that you would like to work on. Then, write down some simple steps that you can take to achieve a greater level of self-mastery in that area.

20
Self-Approval

Self-approval is a combination of self-acceptance and self-support. When you approve of yourself, you don't depend on others to validate you. Instead, you validate yourself by accepting yourself.

Self-Approval Questions For You To Think About

1. Do you fully accept yourself?

2. Do you approve of the way that you live your life currently?

3. Do you approve of who you are as a person?

4. Do you approve of how you allow people to treat you and how you treat others?

5. Do you approve of how you show up for your relationships?

6. Do you tend to seek validation from other people to feel good about yourself or are you able to go against the crowd for something you strongly believe in?

7. Are you overly critical of yourself? (Use the space below to write about it. Then make a mental note to stop being obsessively hard on yourself.)

_____

_____

_____

_____

_____

_____

_____

_____

_____

_____

_____

_____

_____

_____

_____

_____

_____

_____

_____

_____

_____

_____

_____

_____

♥ "The fear of man is a snare, but whoever trusts in the LORD is set securely on high." **Proverbs 29: 25**

21
Self-Preservation

Self-preservation is the 1st law of nature. It's the basic human instinct to protect one's self from hurt, harm and danger. This instinct is also in animals who will attack or run if they feel threatened or sense danger.

Following are some ways that you can self-preserve. Add some additional ways to this list.

1. Learn To Say No

2. Set Boundaries

3. Ask for Help

4. _____

5. _____

6. _____

7. _____

8. _____

9. _____

10.   _____

22
Self-Empowerment

Self-empowerment – is the power within oneself to take full responsibility for your life and then taking action to create the life that you desire. Self-empowerment includes exercising power over your attitude, outlook, emotions and mindset, the power over how you react to people, situations and circumstances as well as the power to take the initiative to do what's necessary for your own betterment and growth.

An example of exercising personal power over your life is making the decision to change an unhealthy behavior or habit. Changing a habit could involve anything from: waking up an hour earlier to work on a goal or dream, giving up smoking, implementing an exercise routine, or controlling an emotional reaction that brings out the worst in you. By quickly and consistently electing to change an unhealthy habit or behavior you get to see your personal power in action.

Think of an area of your life where you desire to exercise greater personal power. In the space below, write down a song, quote, affirmation or scripture to serve as your inspiration to exercise greater personal power in that area of your life.

23
Self-Maintenance

Most people understand the importance of maintenance when it comes to their home, computer, or car. Without proper maintenance these things can break down, or become completely disabled. Well, the same thing happens when we neglect to maintain ourselves: mentally, emotionally, spiritually and physically. While we can easily see the ways that our homes and possessions need maintenance, it's easy to forget that we need "maintenance" for ourselves. It's tempting to rush from one thing to another without reflecting on how we're feeling, whether or not we are eating well, drinking enough water, resting properly and exercising our bodies. However, a little bit of self-maintenance enables us to become more intentional about our health, habits and well-being.

☑ Are there any areas of your life where you have neglected your self-maintenance? Knowing that you only get one body and you want it to serve you well for as long as possible, write down at least 3 things that you can do to practice better self-maintenance.

I Can...

1.

2.

3.

24
Self-Fulfillment

Self-fulfilment also known as personal-fulfillment is the act of fulfilling your heart's desires and life ambitions. Self-fulfillment includes joy, happiness, hope, peace of mind, personal well-being, purpose and your overall vision for your life.

How do you define a fulfilling life? In the space below, jot down some power words in colored pencils/pens that captures your vision of a fulfilling life.

Now that you've jotted down some power words to capture your idea of a fulfilling life, select one or more of your power words and write some ways that you will go about create a more fulfilling life in the space below.

_____

_____

_____

_____

_____

_____

_____

_____

_____

_____

_____

_____

_____

_____

_____

_____

_____

_____

_____

_____

_____

_____

_____

_____

A big part of self-fulfillment also includes making time to do the things that you enjoy, and learning to enjoy your own company.

✍ In the space below write down at least 3 things that you enjoy doing.

✍ In the space below write down simple ways that you can enjoy your own company.

25
Self-Advocacy

Self-advocacy is the ability to speak-up for yourself and advocate for the things that are important to you. Self-advocacy includes asking for what you want and need as well as telling people how you feel when necessary. Self-advocacy also includes setting boundaries and saying "no" when it's necessary. There are 3 parts to becoming an effective **self-advocate.** They are: knowing yourself, knowing your needs, and knowing what steps to take to get what you need or at least put yourself on the right path to get started.

Think about a time in your life when you needed to stand up for yourself or set a clear boundary but you didn't. Knowing what you now know about the 3 parts of self-advocacy, what might you do differently next time you need to speak up for yourself, say no to someone or set a clear boundary?

_____

_____

_____

_____

_____

_____

_____

_____

_____

_____

_____

_____

_____

_____

_____

_____

12 Ways To Practice Self-Love In Your Daily Life

1. Engage in positive self-talk.

2. Surround yourself with people who value you. Stop hanging around people who do not value you.

3. Invest in your personal development.

4. Read books that expand your thinking.

5. Keep your promises to yourself.

6. Get out of your comfort zone.

7. Do things to make you feel proud.

8. Get yourself a composition notebook and write about your achievements and positive qualities.

9. Smile in front of the mirror and be proud of how far you've come.

10. Be intentional about being kind and do at least one random act of kindness every day whenever possible.

11. Write your goals down and pursue them until you achieve them.

12. Spend time doing things that you enjoy.

You Are God's Special Treasure

Deuteronomy 14: 2

You can do all things through Christ who strengthens you
Philippians 4: 13

In Bright Colored Pens or Pencils ...Write Down 5 Affirmations That Make You Feel Really, Really Good

Other Books by Cassandra Mack

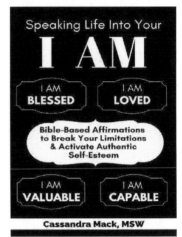

Cassandra Mack's Books are Available @ Amazon.com

Want To Have A Healing Conversation

with Cassandra Mack so that you can gain sustainable strategies that will empower you to facilitate greater success in an area of your life that needs mending & tending to?

Need Wise Guidance & Clear Direction

About An Issue You're Struggling With?

Sign Up for A Strategy Coaching Session

with Cassandra Mack @

StrategiesForEmpoweredLiving.com

Printed in Great Britain
by Amazon

78785129R00038